PATIENT #1

Donald Freed

BROADWAY PLAY PUBLISHING INC
224 E 62nd St, NY, NY 10065
www.broadwayplaypub.com
info@broadwayplaypub.com

PATIENT #1
© Copyright 2007 by Donald Freed

All rights reserved. This work is fully protected under the copyright laws of the United States of America. No part of this publication may be photocopied, reproduced, stored in a retrieval system, or transmitted, in any form or by any means, electronic, mechanical, recording, or otherwise, without the prior permission of the publisher. Additional copies of this play are available from the publisher.

Written permission is required for live performance of any sort. This includes readings, cuttings, scenes, and excerpts. For amateur and stock performances, please contact Broadway Play Publishing Inc. For all other rights please contact the author at pattyraef1@aol.com.

First printing: August 2007
Second printing: October 2007
I S B N: 0-88145-349-8

Book design: Marie Donovan
Word processing: Microsoft Word
Typographic controls: Ventura Publisher
Typeface: Palatino
Printed and bound in the U S A

CHARACTERS & SETTING

DOCTOR, *seventy-four*
PATIENT #1, *sixty-three*
AGENT, *thirty*

Time: December-January 2009-2010

Place: An elite psychiatric clinic in south Florida

The first production of PATIENT #1 will be in the Spring of 2008 at York Theatre Royal (Artistic Director, Damian Cruden).

The first U S production will be in Autumn 2008 at the Odyssey Theater, Los Angeles (Artistic Director, Ron Sossi).

MISE-EN-SCENE

PATIENT #1 is the confidential in-patient, designated in-house name assigned to the former President of the United States George W Bush by the psychiatric staff of an elite private clinic.

The clinic is isolated from and virtually unknown to the public. The clientele over the years has included some of America's and the world's most Very Important Persons. The style and spirit of the large office in which the action takes place is deluxe Spanish *Modernismo* circa 1930.

There are two entrances, stage left (S L) and stage right (S R).

A large desk/table is center left; a fireplace, left; and a small table, chair and couch center right. Almost the entire upstage wall is a picture window.

Through the window can be seen a wide lush lawn, semi-tropical flowers, vegetation and, at the horizon, a flash of ocean. The sound of waves is constant but very far away. Also, in the distance, the ringing of an old mission's bells.

AUTHOR'S NOTE

PATIENT #1 became an international reality when Damian Cruden of York Theatre Royal, and Ron Sossi of the Los Angeles Odyssey Theater, together with Professors Ron Marasco, Chair of Theater at Loyola Marymount University, and Jon Farris, Emeritus Chair of Theater Arts at Denison University—when all of these notable American and British artists combined to prepare the play for production in the fateful American election year of 2008.

The first reading of the work was held in Los Angeles by Cinda Jackson at her Lost Studio Theater in the spring of 2006. In November 2006, a staged reading followed in the Workshop Theatre at the University of Leeds.

At Leeds, the brilliant Artistic Director of York Theatre Royal, Damian Cruden, signalled his interest in what was bound to be a problematic project, given the toxic relationship of the U S and the U K in the Middle Eastern disasters of Mr Bush.

Damian Cruden's response to any political problems the work might provoke was to argue for a U K/U S co-production with tours in England and America! This vision of courage and creativity is the hallmark of Mr Cruden, and when Ron Sossi, Ron Marasco, and Jon Farris learned of the plan they travelled to England, by plane and e-mail, and the deal was done!

The important Mercury Theatre in Colchester, England, joined Damian Cruden to help sponsor the U K tour.

We all believed, with Matthew Arnold, that "The Theatre is Revolutionary, organize the Theatre!" We also know that this U K/U S combination would constitute a new theater entity and that a "New Theatre", in Albert Camus' words, "changes History". And, finally, what choice did we have, since we were each of us seized of Antonin Artaud's dictum that "We are not free and the sky can still fall on our heads and the Theatre has been created to teach us that first of all".

We believed all of this. We always had—and I trust we always will.

This play is dedicated to Damian Cruden, Ron Sossi, Jon Farris, Ron Marasco, and Charles Erven: the artists who had the courage and the large talents needed to tell the truth in the United Kingdom and the United States. And to Christopher "Kip" Gould, the bravest and best of publishers. But, above all, to Patricia Freed.

ACT ONE

(Overture. A sound capsule of the Bush years: 2000-2008)

Scene One

(A brilliant December morning, 10 A M. Birdsong, ocean waves)

(A security AGENT *runs past, outside the U S picture window. The* AGENT *is dressed in a tailored dark grey suit and wears black sunglasses. As he trots, the* AGENT *mutters into a miniaturized cell phone.)*

(In the quiet can be heard birdsong, waves and the beat of a helicopter chopping in, then out.)

(The DOCTOR *enters his office from left. He moves in quick angry bursts, cursing under his breath. He sets down his topcoat and a small suitcase; studies his desk and office, curses.)*

DOCTOR: Sonofabitch. *(He forces himself to stop, to breathe, to regain control, then very deliberately he exits with the coat and suitcase.)*

(The DOCTOR *re-enters with a box of Kleenex and a bowl of candy, still fighting for control.)*

(He wears expensive Brooks Brother's slacks and a cashmere sweater, a blue oxford shirt, an "old school" tie, and loafers. He reacts to the sound and shadow of the helicopter, waits for

it to pass, listens to bells from a distant mission, then goes to work, muttering epithets, again.)

(The sound of a motorbike passing by out of sight breaks the quiet. Then stillness again)

(At his desk, the psychoanalyst fumes over a case file, then reaches toward a small tape machine. He reaches, then reacts to the sight of his hand shaking; pulls back, bows his head, shuts his eyes—centers his powers of intention, initiates a yoga breathing exercise, and tries again.

(DOCTOR reads file on desk. Then, speaks into tape machine.)

DOCTOR: Wednesday, December 17— *(He breaks off, once again, to take command of his rage...)* Wednesday, December 17, 2009...I am reading from the cover-sheet of a file, page roman numeral one, dated December 8, 2009...mmm...the heading, ah, is, ah—it indicates that the file, this file, has been generated by, um, quotes, "Homeland Security, colon: Distribution Eyes Only, colon: ah, F B I; C I A; D I A; D E A; N I H; O N I; S S; G 2; J C S; C I D; N S A; M I 6; and, ah...five other acronyms that I do not recognize..."Eyes Only". And every other line, every line and every word on this covering page has been redacted. Completely blacked out! ..."Eyes Only"...

(The DOCTOR stops recording. He leans his head on his hand and stares hollow eyed, blindly, in to space. Then he closes his eyes. Re-opens them. Breaths. Performs a yoga exercise and chants a mantra in order to revive himself:)

DOCTOR ...Ooo-ne-ma-ne-pad-ne-ooommmm... *(Repeated three times; building in resonance, until he is prepared to resume recording:)* December 17, 2009, continued...in my absence, I have— *(Stops the tape, breaths , starts again)* Mm, while I was travelling— *(Stops, starts)* I have, emm, returned to find a, quote, "Legat 405 Order", close quotes, from the Department of Homeland Security, quotes, "Remanding", close

quotes, a certain, quotes, "Citizen of the United States
of America", close quotes, to the quotes, "Custody
of the above-named..." etc, etc. Concluding that—
(He stands, reading.) That the said, quotes, "citizen",
is, quotes, "Hereinafter referenced in the above-named
category as, quotes *(Stops, curses silently, starts again)*
"Patient Number 1." Close quotes.

(The DOCTOR *walks slowly to the door, right, and peers into
the darkness. Then he goes into a corner, lowers his voice,
and resumes his recording.)*

DOCTOR: Wednesday December 17, 2009, continue:
Am I to understand that during my absence and before
I have examined the instant case file of this so-called
"Patient Number 1," a "protected client" —that
someone has put this man on a psychotropic regime
that includes: Valium, Xanax, Lorizipam, Effexsor,
Prolixin, Zoloft, Paxzil, Lithium, Zyprexa, Haldol, and
sonofabitch, Uroxadal?! And that this has been done
without any consultation with me—to a Patient who is
mute, of whom you write, quotes, he may be feigning
an autistic state, close quotes—and that there is, quotes,
"the possibility of a deception—"

*(A knock at the door. At the sound of a tap on the door, right.
The* DOCTOR *clicks off the tape. The* DOCTOR *crosses to the
door, right, and opens it to the security* AGENT. *The Two
men stand in the doorway for a moment—suddenly The*
AGENT *darts into the* DOCTOR's *office: circles, inspects,
and races out again.)*

*(The physician is further outraged, then staggered at what he
sees coming toward him and in to the office doorway:)*

(The AGENT *backs in leading* PATIENT #1 *with hand signals
and body language, the way an airport technician signals
directions to a plane as it taxis on the tarmac. In the doorway,
the* AGENT *smoothes the* PATIENT's *hair and straightens his
bath robe. The psychoanalyst stares as the* AGENT *uses more*

hand signals and gestures to, literally, guide the PATIENT
through the doorway and into the office.)

*(The ex-President is almost robotic, paralysed by conflicting
waves of fear and need.)*

DOCTOR: *(Sotto voce)* My God...

*(The ex-President wears a robe and slippers; his hair is long
and grey, his face is covered with stubble; he is heavily
medicated; and yet he continues to attempt to walk as he
did in public life—the cowboy hero with the bulging biceps,
the brass balls, the stiff fingers—a caricature of machismo
twice over.)*

(To top off this mad apparition, the PATIENT *has a bandage
plastered across his temple. The* DOCTOR *tries to peer past
the* AGENT *to catch the* PATIENT'*s eye, but each time the
inmate shifts his head to avoid the analyst's probing gaze.)*

DOCTOR: Thank You.

(Pause. The AGENT *takes a step toward the* DOCTOR,
who stops him with)

DOCTOR: Please wait.

(The AGENT *hesitates, looks at both men, then backs out,
speaking into his wire:)*

AGENT: ..."Ranch Hand" at eleven hundred hours—
do you copy? —That's a Roger—negative—negative—
(Off) —negative...

(The AGENT *stays just outside the door, watching. Silence.
The* PATIENT *stares like a heavily medicated statue, drooling
slightly.)*

DOCTOR: Make yourself at home...

(The PATIENT *stands fixed. The* DOCTOR *studies him,
noting the small bandage on the* PATIENT'*s temple.
He steps closer to examine the bandage.)*

DOCTOR: ...Mm... They tell me you're quite a bike racer. *(Pause)* Dirt bike, is it?

(The DOCTOR*'s voice and diction is well bred, mid-Atlantic. Pause. He reaches to inspect the bandage, the* PATIENT *jerks his head back. The* DOCTOR *retreats several steps. A helicopter sound in and out. Silence)*

DOCTOR: Keeps you fit, does it? And they tell me you're making good use of the "Fitness Center." So, you're, ah, comfortable, quite comfortable here—are you? *(Pause)* Runs in the family, eh? Your dad—parachuted from a plane on his, what?, eightieth birthday? Quite a man. *(Pause)* "Healthy mind in a healthy body"? It's a good old saying.

(The DOCTOR *takes a step closer. Silence. Suddenly the psychoanalyst reaches down and tries to shake the* PATIENT*'s hand. The* PATIENT *stiffens in terror, but cannot extricate his hand. The* DOCTOR *grips and holds on as he talks; the two men are locked in a stationary* agon, *an immobile wrestling match. Why is the cowboy he-man no match for the older care giver? Is the* PATIENT *trying to pull away or, secretly, clinging to the medicine man?)*

The DOCTOR *pumps and jerks the* PATIENT*'s hand. Trying to throw the ex-leader off balance, testing for a deception.)*

DOCTOR: A great honor to meet you in person, again, sir... Almost ten years. Palm Beach... Well... Looking forward to working, ah, working together... Chopping wood—ha-ha—teamwork, ah, yes, clearing brush— Ha! —I remember hearing you say, ah, on television, once, that, ah—when you—it struck me— When you and the Vice-President were questioned, ah, together, in "executive session", is that the phrase? —After the first attack on New York—that you—and you insisted that the two of you face them together—the Commission—that you wanted it that way—President and Vice-President together—so that, ah, I think you put it, so that "they," the committee, could, ah, "see our body language." Was that it? Your body language—a-ha...

(Just as suddenly, the DOCTOR *lets go. But the inmate clings to the* DOCTOR's *wrist! The medico is shaken, as is the* AGENT *watching behind his dark glasses. The* AGENT *signals and begins his backwards ushering out of the drooling* PATIENT, *leaving the* DOCTOR *staring in deep confusion at his own wrist, as the sick man's grasp finally loosens and he is led away.)*

(The DOCTOR *stares after them. Silence. The loud ignition of the dirt bike cracks through the office and the police dogs bark.)*

DOCTOR: Son-of-a-bitch!

(The DOCTOR *stares out, lost in the horror of the situation.... Again, he seeks relief in a yoga exercise, then makes a telephone call. Again, his hand trembles as he picks up the receiver; he wills himself to dial.)*

DOCTOR: *(Raising his voice)* ...Good morning... Is she available? ...Mother—hello—I'm back—yes, I'm here... Well, I'm here... Mmm— No, I'll call *you*— Yes— No, I'll call *you*— Can't talk now—*Cannot talk now!* We cannot talk! —What? ...I can't—hello, Mother— Can you— Can you hear me now? —Hello? There's something— Mother? —Something wrong— Mother? *Something wrong!*

(The motor bike cracks back across the day, drowning out the DOCTOR, *plunging the room into darkness.)*

Scene Two

*(In darkness the bike reverberations fade into the sound
of a storm.)*

*(Lights up on a storm scene: 10 A M the next day.
The* DOCTOR *is turning on lamps in the office.
He goes to his desk and begins to dictate.)*

*(A roll of thunder, and another sound coming closer
the dirt bike.)*

(The DOCTOR *listens, waits for the noise to pass then
dictates. He stands warming himself before a low fire,
as he speaks into a small portable microphone.)*

DOCTOR: ...Thursday December 18, 2009: Regarding
Patient Number One: Am I to understand that the client
has permission to continue riding his machine, despite
the extraordinary level of his medication and the clear
and present danger to—

(The DOCTOR *breaks off as* PATIENT *and the security*
AGENT, *wearing complete rain gear, run past the U S
window. The* AGENT *runs backwards, as always, holding
a black umbrella to shield his master.)*

DOCTOR: The client is in the hacienda, as we speak—
the extreme danger! Unthinkable that I should, that the
Clinic should be placed in this position— *(He lowers his
voice)* with a client who has a notorious reputation as
a prankster and a provocateur who for all we know
may be here to create some kind of deception *(a knock
on door)* to be used as a defense before some future
national or international tribunal—

(Another knock at the door. The DOCTOR *stops his dictation,
breathes deeply, performs a quick yoga exercise, and goes to
open the door.)*

DOCTOR: Please come in.

(PATIENT *and the security* AGENT *enter dripping wet. The* DOCTOR *signals the* AGENT *to leave. Instead, the* AGENT *wipes rain off the* PATIENT. *The* PATIENT *stands, again, in his frozen posture.*)

DOCTOR: Will you take off your slicker and stand over here in front of the fire?

(*The* PATIENT *is locked in his pose. The* DOCTOR *tries but still cannot get past the* AGENT *to look the client in the eye. Thunder and lightning, and then heavy rain.*)

DOCTOR: Family coming down for Christmas?

(*Rain. The* DOCTOR *moves closer, the* PATIENT *is shaking.*)

DOCTOR: You have a chill.

(*The* PATIENT'*s shaking becomes violent.*)

DOCTOR: Please take the patient to the infirmary.

(*The* AGENT *stares.*)

DOCTOR: Soldier, this man is shaking with ague.

(AGENT *stares*)

DOCTOR: Do you understand English?! —Take the man out of here! To the nurse.

(*The* AGENT *backs the* PATIENT *out. The* DOCTOR *follows.*)

DOCTOR: —Then come straight back! I'll call Mrs Gonzales.

DOCTOR: (*On telephone*) ...*Señora*—*problema:* Patient Number One is on his way to you, now. —*Numero Uno. Muy importante:* get a Doctor, and a *witness*, and find out—*momento*—whether or not he is actually as ill as he seems or whether he is...*Exactamente!* —"faking"! (*Lights flicker*) And then call me directly. Not the Doctor. You!

(The storm builds again and the lights flicker and fade to black as he talks.)

Scene Three

(In the dark the storm fades to a dripping silence. Lights up on an overcast scene, thirty minutes later. Mission bells in distance)

(The security AGENT *stands in the doorway. The* DOCTOR *sits listening to someone on the telephone.)*

DOCTOR: ...*Bueno. (He hangs up. Pause)* They'll keep him overnight for observation...Let's review the bidding, Mister, ah, Mister Coe, is it? John Coe?

AGENT: Yes, sir. Affirmative.

DOCTOR: Sit Down. You came in day and date with the, ah, Patient?

AGENT: Roger. *(He does not sit.)*

DOCTOR: *(Pause)* Is "Coe" your actual, ah—in other words, is "John Coe" your "John Doe".

(Pause. Then the AGENT *turns to leave.)*

DOCTOR: One moment.

AGENT: Sir.

DOCTOR: Where you going?

AGENT: I can't leave him. *(Pause)*

DOCTOR: You're S S, aren't you?

AGENT: Repeat?

DOCTOR: S S—Secret Service. You came here with him—you work for him, or his family, or the government, or somebody.

AGENT: That's a Roger.

DOCTOR: Somebody other than this clinic?

(The AGENT *salutes smartly, wheels and exits.)*

DOCTOR: *(Shouting)* Is that a "Roger"?!

(The DOCTOR *goes to window, studies the sky—cursing under his breath—then a yoga exercise, and then to telephone. Christmas music rising under.)*

DOCTOR: *(On telephone)* Hello. I need a boat for Key Largo.

(Christmas music up, lights down as a New Year's crowd sings Auld Lang Syne *and voices call out "Happy New Year 2010!")*

Scene Four

(Early January, 2010, 10 A M. Tableau: AGENT *in doorway;* PATIENT *in his rigid pose;* DOCTOR *watching, standing center. Bright sunlight and birdsong)*

DOCTOR: Happy New Year, Gentlemen. *(To* PATIENT*)* Feeling better? How's the head? ...They tell me you watched all the games... Big turkey dinner. First class chef, *El Jefé*; all the, ah, "trimmings." Food agree with you? *(Pause)* Mister Coe?

AGENT: Repeat.

DOCTOR: Is the, ah, "chow" to your specifications?

AGENT: Affirmative.

DOCTOR: "American Plan." *(To the Patient)* Well—shall we sit down and put our feet up? *(Silence)* Shall we start the ball rolling with a little New Year's chat? *(Silence)* Mister Coe, I have to step out for a minute. Please have the patient seated when I return. *(Pause)* Otherwise I will be leaving. —I will disappear. *Desaparacido.* —I will be gone!

(The DOCTOR *exits, left. Silence. The* AGENT *breathes heavily, in deep conflict. Finally, he tries to back the* PATIENT *to the settee, Down right. But as the* AGENT *attempts to seat the ex-Commander in Chief, the* PATIENT *continues to follow his warder so that they make a complete circle around the couch. At last the agent manages to "drop off" the* PATIENT *on the couch.)*

(The sick man sits staring up at the AGENT, *like a lost child. The* DOCTOR *now stands in the doorway watching.)*

DOCTOR: Thank you...You may leave, now.

(Pause. The AGENT *exits. The* PATIENT *looks after him, his eyes remain fixed on the open door.)*

(The DOCTOR *brings a chair and sits near the* PATIENT.*)*

DOCTOR: ...He's a fine young man. And he cares about you. We all do... You were pretty sick, there, for about a week, weren't you? —But you're completely restored now. Mrs Gonzales took good care of you. I was in touch with her every day... Can you look at me, sir? Your, ah, S S man will be coming back in a few minutes...I'll call him—if you'll look at me.

(Very slowly the PATIENT *turns his head an inch or two toward the* DOCTOR *but does not make eye contact.)*

DOCTOR: That's good, that's champion. Thank you. I'll call Mister Coe back now—in just a few minutes.

(The DOCTOR *takes a candy for himself and offers one to the Patient. No response)*

DOCTOR: No? These were President Reagan's favourite brand. You looked up to Mister Reagan—you wrote in your book—you remember your book? —called him by his nickname—when you were a lad—used to call him the "Gipper" —remember? —and "The Big Guy"? *(He leans in, his voice warm and concerned.)* You knew them all. Quite a life. You wrote that you had "all the

luck"—in your book... And now this, hmm? ...But you
have time ahead of you, a lot of time, and a great many
people out there, like Mister Coe, who still believe in
you. You have the rest of your life waiting for you.
Think of your stay here as just the, ah, "half-time", uh,
rest period. Then back out on the field. You leading the
cheers—like always—like at Andover—like at Yale.

(The PATIENT *reacts—slightly to the word "Yale". The*
DOCTOR *leans in.)*

DOCTOR: Good old Yale...I'll tell you a secret: You and
I have some things in common. Can you guess? Shall I
give you a hint?

(Pause. The DOCTOR *hums a phrase of the Yale*
Whiffenpoof *song. The* PATIENT *reacts making a*
small plosive "P" sound four or five times:)

PATIENT: P-P-P-P

DOCTOR: Yale '57—that's me. Same fraternity, too, same
as you, D K E. You see? I was a "Deke"', so we can talk,
Yale-Man to Yale-Man...I was a Deke, like you, except
they made you President of the House. But I know the
drill, all the secrets. Hm, didn't we burn D K E, in
Greek, *Delta Kappa Epsilon*, burn it into the new boys'
butts with cigarette, ah, butts, hmm, "Rite of Passage",
that sort of thing? But your year got caught, '68, and
The New York Times called it "torture" in a headline—
I have the clippings, here—and you were suspended—
temporarily—but you fought back, said it was all just
"Yale Tradition" —and so it was, so it was. And your
Dad, he stood by you, and your mother, especially your
mother. So, we were both Deke-Men, but I had the
good luck to be there in the fifties. But the one who
had it all was your father, the golden boy, in the forties.
Now, those were the days—raccoon coats, ukuleles,
white bucks... So let's talk Deke-Man to Deke-Man,
Yale-Man to Yale-Man. And—I have a little treat to

share with you. *(Leans in)* I have a tape of "Rudy Valle
and his Boys"—their original recording. Way before
your time, but when you were a cheerleader in '68 you
used to play that record for all the Deke new boys—
we all did—when you were the Deke-in-Chief. Hm?
You ready? You remember? Yale? "Skull and Bones"?
You remember. *(He goes to his desk to turn on the prepared
tape cut.)* Ready:

*(Out pours the scratchy sentiment, in all its adolescent
power, of Rudy Valle and his Band. The* DOCTOR *hums
along softly, tries to encourage the* PATIENT, *but the*
PATIENT *only stares away, into the past, and makes the
small, tight popping "P" sounds.)*

To the tables down at Mory's
To the place where Louis dwells
To the dear old Temple Bar we love so well
Sing the Whiffenpoofs assembled
With their glasses raised on high
And the magic of their singing casts its spell

Yes, the magic of their singing
Of the songs we love so well
'shall I Wasting,' and 'Mavourneen', and the rest
We will serenade our Louis while life and voice shall
    last
Then we'll pass and be forgotten with the rest

We're poor little lambs who have lost our way
Baa! Baa! Baa!
We're little black sheep who have gone astray
Baa! Baa! Baa!

Gentleman songsters off on a spree
Damned from here to eternity
God have mercy on such as we
Baa! Baa! Baa!

(The DOCTOR *stops the tape after the first time through.)*

DOCTOR: "Little black sheep"... You're a little black sheep, who's gone astray—that's all...so let's sing one verse for old times sake, shall we? You and I... You and your Dad. He and his Dad. All of us. All the way back.

(*The* DOCTOR *resumes the recording, sings along, but the* PATIENT *only stares. The* DOCTOR, *head to head with him, thinks he sees a tear on the younger man's cheek.*)

(*The music plays out. Silence. The* DOCTOR *studies* PATIENT, *who, again, makes the tiny "P" sound. Then, the* DOCTOR, *signals for the* AGENT. *The* AGENT *enters. The* AGENT, *guides the* PATIENT *out. As he exits, the ex-leader cranks up his cowboy caricature of a body image, as usual.*)

DOCTOR: (*To* AGENT) You come right back.

(AGENT *exits.*)

DOCTOR: (*Into tape*) January 4th 2009, uh, 2010—*2010.* Immediate suicide watch indicated for Patient Number One. However, no further increase—repeat, no increase—of medication dosage.

(*He switches back to the "Whiffenpoof" tape. Listens for a minute, a deep sigh.*)

DOCTOR: Son-of-a-bitch. (*Turns tape off. Takes off his glasses. With profound irony he recalls and sings an old school parody of the song:*)

DOCTOR: Bright college days... Ivy covered professors in ivy covered walls... To-o-o the tables down at Mory's (where ever that may be)... We will cut all our classes and cheat on our exams, and we'll "pass" and be forgotten with the rest.

(*The analyst is wounded, lost in memory... The* AGENT *appears in the doorway. The two men stare at each other...helicopter over and out.*)

DOCTOR: He needs our help now.

AGENT: Repeat?

DOCTOR: *(Pause)* He wept.

AGENT: *(Pause)* Repeat.

DOCTOR: He wept... He's a person... Do you understand what I'm telling you? —I would not vote for the man at gun point, but he is a person. Do you copy, Mister Coe?

AGENT: *(Pause) A* person?

(The AGENT *always pronounces the article as a long A.)*

DOCTOR: A Person. A *Homo sapiens.*

DOCTOR: Negative!

DOCTOR: A human being...

AGENT: *A* human being?

DOCTOR: That's a Roger.

*(*Whiffenpoof *song, under, as lights fade.)*

(A time montage: January 7, 8, & 9, 2010)

(Three scenes, January 7, 8, 9—2010. The DOCTOR *announces the date of each scene into his tape.)*

(There is low thunder and rain.)

(In each separate scene, the DOCTOR *studies the* PATIENT. *The* PATIENT *is always mute, except for the "P— P— P—" sounds that he makes.)*

(In the third scene. January 9, 2010, the therapist breaks the excruciating silence to try an experiment: he sings a verse and chorus of the old Christian hymn, Leaning On The Everlasting Arms.*)*

(The result is, again, nothing. Silence and rain)

Scene Eight

DOCTOR: *(Voiceover)* January 11, 2010.

(The day is overcast at 10 A M. The PATIENT is, again, seated; staring. The DOCTOR is at his desk watching and listening to the barely audible pops from the PATIENT.)

(Morning sounds including far away ocean waves. Unobserved, the clinician takes a series of photographs of the lunatic from various angles...)

PATIENT: -P-P-P;-P-P-P-

(Then, the DOCTOR picks up a children's book from his desk and moves with stealth behind the PATIENT.)

(The analyst holds the book in front of the staring inmate and reads softly into his right ear, as if to a child.)

(As the DOCTOR reads, the outer office door opens silently and the Secret Service AGENT's head eases into view. He stares and spies.)

DOCTOR: ...Ah, now the three bears walked through the kitchen and into the bedroom and, ah...and the Mama Bear said, "Somebody's been sleeping in my bed and it's..."

(DOCTOR quickly switches over to confide a message into the PATIENT's left ear.)

DOCTOR: —Sir. Mister President. Sir, CINCON is reporting a plane crashing into the New York World Trade Center—Sir?

(The DOCTOR switches back to PATIENT's right ear.)

DOCTOR: —Then the Papa Bear said, "Look, someone's been lying in my—"

(Quick switch back to PATIENT's left ear.)

DOCTOR: Sir! —Sir! CINPAC confirms a second plane's crashed into the World Trade Center—Sir!

(Back to right ear)

DOCTOR: —And the Baby Bear cried, *"And there he is!"*

(Is something happening? The clinician is up on tip-toes... But the PATIENT *only stares and makes his sound. All three men peer out toward the audience, into the distance.)*

PATIENT: P-P-P-P...

(The DOCTOR *whirls and flexes to hurl the book against the wall. To contain his fury he freezes into a statue. Thus, statuesque, he meets the gaze of the Secret Service* AGENT, *whose protruding head stares, then slowly disappears...)*

(Then, the physician breaths again and drops the book into the waste basket; brings a chair over and sits next to the prisoner.)

(Church bells in the distance.)

PATIENT: P-P-P- ; P-P-P-

DOCTOR: I believe, sir, that you are trying to say something. Some other people around here think that you're, ah, "taking the piss," as we say in England, taking the piss out of me and the staff by playing little games and riding your bike at speed—but I don't. And so, today, I'm going to toss you some words and I want you to sling any answer or idea you get from my words right back to me. You simply say the first thing that comes into your mind, and don't censor yourself. Remember: no one—can control—their thoughts—so don't even try.

(The PATIENT *appears half asleep. The* DOCTOR *picks up a clip board from his desk.)*

DOCTOR: Ready? "Shock and Awe"..."Guantanamo"... "Skull and Bones"...

(The PATIENT *appears to be asleep. The* DOCTOR *rises and begins to pace. He lifts his voice.)*

DOCTOR: "Abu Ghraib"…"Waterboarding"… "Torture"…"White phosphorous"—"Shake and Bake"…"Osama Bin Laden"…"The World Court"…"Hate Crimes"…"Democracy"

*(*PATIENT *snores. The* DOCTOR *crosses off words—muttering:)*

DOCTOR: "Gay Marriage", "Virgin Mary", "Organ Failure".

(The DOCTOR *kneels and confides into the* PATIENT's *ear.)*

DOCTOR: …"Buddy", your dead pup "Buddy"… "Pappy"…"Mammy"

*(*PATIENT *sticks out his tongue)*

DOCTOR: "Pappy and Mammy" *(He checks off more words…)* "Dick Cheney"…"Body Language"…"Dick's body language"…"Al Gore"…"Bill Clinton"…"Hilary Clinton"…"Hilary Clinton's body language"…"Electric Shock"…"Rendition"…"Abortion"…"Cocaine"…"Ghost Detainees"…"Taking the gloves off"…"Pump and Dump"…"Lebanon, the Cedars of Lebanon, the destruction of Lebanon…"

(The DOCTOR *tries to contain his frustration. The* PATIENT *makes low vomit sounds and sticks his tongue out whenever his mother is mentioned. In response to other words he snores or pops his Ps.)*

DOCTOR: "Date Rape"…"Bush Exploration", "Arbusto Energy", "Spectrum 7", "Enron", "Harken Oil" —and all your other bankruptcies! You're perspiring, sir—so am I… *(Louder)* "9/11"…"2/13 and the Second Attack on Chicago"…"Anthrax"…the late "Saddam Hussein"… "Dick Cheney", the late "Dick Cheney" *(Snores)* —wake up, son…"Hurricane Katrina"…"Barbara Bush"…"John

F Kennedy"..."Lee Harvey
Oswald"..."Iraq"..."Iran"..."MalcolmX"..."The
Black Panthers"..."Barbara Bush!"..."Capital
Punishment"!..."*Family!*"..."FLORIDA—FAMILY!"
(Dancing with frustration) ...Terror...Ter/ror—
Remem/ber Ter/ror? *The Cheapest Word in the English
language! (He swears furiously to himself, draws the drapes
closed and shouts—)* Wake up, boy! Tomorrow's the big
game!

(The PATIENT *starts, makes the "P" popping sound,
louder now.)*

PATIENT: P— P— P—

DOCTOR: Damn straight. You Yell Leaders get moving
now. Ready? Let's go.

(The DOCTOR *vocally mimes stadium crowd sounds and
band marching music.)*

PATIENT: P— P— P—

DOCTOR: C'mon you Dekes, it's game time!

(The DOCTOR *starts into a cheerleader routine in a an urgent
effort to mobilize the* PATIENT.*)*

DOCTOR: *(Singing to band music)*
Bingo, Bingo,
Bingo, Bingo, Bingo,
That's the lingo,
Eli is bound to win!...
C'mon, kid, let's hear it! "Rah-Rah-Siss-Boom-Bah!"
(He sings and laughs in pain.)
Bah! Bah! Bah! -Ha-Ha-Ha!

*(*DOCTOR *tries to lift* PATIENT *to his feet.)*

PATIENT: P— P— P—

DOCTOR: Good, that's it, that's champion. You
cheerleaders, altogether now!
...When the sons of Eli break through the line,

That is the sign we hail,
Bull-dog! Bull-dog! Bow, wow, wow,
Eli Yale!

(The DOCTOR *sinks down, spent. The* PATIENT *sits staring out:)*

PATIENT: P—P—P *(He Makes his sound in the silence.)*

*(*DOCTOR *goes to door, brings in the lurking* AGENT, *gestures them out. Silence. Alone, the* DOCTOR *tries to recover. Then, he stares out and attempts to imitate the* PATIENT's *popping "P" sounds. Tries again, racking his brain: Remembers hand shaking routine with* PATIENT *in first scene—acts it out:)*

DOCTOR: P— P— P..."

(The DOCTOR, *now, tries walking and standing like the* PATIENT—*suddenly he sits in the* PATIENT's *chair in No. 1's posture, hands over crotch.)*

DOCTOR: "P— P— P— P"... What? What does it mean?

(The DOCTOR's *entire body arches with his effort to penetrate the secret of* PATIENT:)*

DOCTOR: "P— P— P": Pappy, Poppy: P— P— P..."

(Then he tries:)

DOCTOR: "P-uppy," and "P-lease," and "Stop," and "Please Stop"...

(The depth psychologist, on the rack of his memory and his life—suddenly the meaning of the secret breaks through—like an electric shock—and his hair stands on end, his flesh shivers up in bumps. He sinks down into himself. Tears run down his cheeks. PATIENT's *voice breaks out of his, the* DOCTOR's, *mouth, in a final shaking sob on the last "Help.")*

DOCTOR: "P—P—P...HelP, HelP, HelP..."

END OF ACT ONE

ACT TWO

Scene One

(Early January, 2010; 11 P M. The DOCTOR *and the* AGENT *enter the office from opposite doors, L and R. The* AGENT *wears a T-shirt and a shoulder holster, no coat and tie. He is barefoot. Low thunder)*

(Cold moonlight bathes the DOCTOR's *office. A low fire burns on the hearth. The* DOCTOR *turns on two lamps, still leaving deep shadows.)*

DOCTOR: Sit down. I had to wake you. Is he sleeping?

AGENT: Affirmative.

DOCTOR: Does he sleep? *(Pause)* How does he sleep? ...Does he walk in his sleep? —Sit down, please.

(Bells from the Old Mission in the distance. The AGENT *stands.)*

DOCTOR: The Old Mission... Are we Catholic?

AGENT: Repeat?

DOCTOR: You Catholic?

AGENT: ...Decline to state.

DOCTOR: Quite right... So, *does* he—walk in his sleep?

AGENT: Negative.

DOCTOR: No? How do you know? Do you sleep?

AGENT: Affirmative.

DOCTOR: With him? In the same suite? On the floor?

AGENT: Affirmative.

DOCTOR: On a pallet. I know. *(Pause)* Does the patient *talk* in his sleep?

AGENT: Negative.

DOCTOR: And you'd know, wouldn't you? Because you're right there, with your gun next to you on the rug, and you'd hear him, and you'd be up and moving in the moonlight and—

AGENT: That's a—

DOCTOR: That's a Roger—and you'd check him out, and tuck him in if he were—

AGENT: That's a—

DOCTOR: That's an affirmative—because, in fact, he does "talk". He makes sounds—like this, "P— P— P" ...That's a fact, isn't it, officer? I've read his lips. —Sit down, officer. That's an order.

(The AGENT stares. Compromises: "sits" without actually touching the chair with his body. They stare. Ocean waves, distant)

DOCTOR: He talks. That's an affirmative fact. A fact. A true fact. The truth. That's why I insisted you drop in tonight. The truth. The time has come for the truth. *(Pause)* " P—P—P—." You know what that means? *(Pause)* He's calling for help: "HelP—HelP—HelP"... And that's what we're going to do. You and I, we're going to help him. Before it's too late... You know why we're going to help him? ...Because if we don't—save him—he's going to die—because we will have to kill him.

AGENT: *(Leaping up)* Negative.

DOCTOR: "Negative." In the extreme. Because when he dies—don't move—when we *let* him die— They are going to come here to get us—you and me—and the photographs of the three dead bodies will flash around the world: his, and yours, and mine. And they will I D you as John Coe A K A John Doe A K A Richard Roe and, then, they'll add on one more name—a long one—that includes the cognates "Abu", and "Ben", and "Ali", and "Muhammad"...Muhammad... And I'll be revealed as a "terrorist sleeper agent, known to the authorities as "Doctor Death" ...End of fable... You may have noticed that none of the staff returned after the New Year break. Except for the nurse and kitchen crew, and they'll be gone the day after tomorrow. And we'll be here all alone. Just the three of us. The three bears. So—sit down, John Doe, and I'll brief you. *(Speaking into the* AGENT'*s ear)* A) He's a moral idiot. B) He's being medicated to death. Shh! And if I cut out his meds he could go berserk—homicide, suicide—so either way, we'll be blamed. You and me... Now, sit down.

AGENT: ...Are you *a* U S citizen?

(Silence. The AGENT *does not move. The* DOCTOR *takes off his glasses, rubs his eyes, sighs deeply, and sits.)*

DOCTOR: It's late.... "P— P— P... Help." We're going to help him because he's been a sleepwalker all his life. Never had a chance. They—the "Family" and the "Friends" —they stuffed those chants and those cheers and that fake Texas accent in his mouth and they hard-wired him to steal the Presidency, steal the country, steal what's left of the world's oil, and then this kleptocracy of kin folk programmed him to kill himself on that goddamn bike of his at Camp Victory— except that their perfect puppet started to actually believe the word salad that they had force fed him all those years, and he somehow got it into his tortured— I say "tortured" —reptilian brain that for some

inscrutable reason Jesus Christ did not want him
to die— You were there, Mister Doe. You saw it
happening— You were there when he refused to
retire to the ranch, and they were compelled to hustle
him into a certain lobbyist's private jet—with just a
"special-ops nurse", a *Dick and Jane* fourth grade reader,
a copy of *The Three Bears*, and you, yourself, Mister
Roe—and brought him here to kill himself.

(The AGENT *lurches to his feet.)*

AGENT: Negative!

(The DOCTOR *rises: face to face.)*

DOCTOR: Kill himself, sir! Make him a martyr.
Concentration Camps *(Sings)* "from California to
the New York Island." *(Pause)* You took an oath,
Mister Coe, to "preserve, protect and defend" this
country and this man. Affirmative? You did. So did I.
Well—America, the America we thought we lived in,
is no more—America is—

AGENT: America—is—

DOCTOR: No more. She died. She broke down and she
died... Look at me... What am I doing?

(The psychiatrist reaches for AGENT'*s dark glasses. Rebuffed,
he, then, mimes a cowboy drawing and firing two six-guns.
But the "cowboy's" knees are shaking in extreme fear.)*

DOCTOR: Do you copy, Mister Coe? —Watch again...
This little act is the new universal symbol for the U S A,
for our country: extreme aggression, extreme fear.
Pathological, infantile paroxysms of homicidal rage
and panic. —Watch again, cowboy... You understand,
at last, what we've become?

AGENT: *(Pause)* Negative.

DOCTOR: In psychiatry we call that answer a "A
Psychoanalytic Yes"... She's dying, America, she's

dying, but I can't treat her in this clinic—I can only treat *him*, and, with your aid, sir, that is what I intend to do. Do you copy? Shhhh. Don't answer yet. You took an oath, you swore on a Bible, that you believe in word for word, to give your life for him, didn't you?

AGENT: *(A whisper)* Roger.

DOCTOR: Roger. And you're willing to die for him here and now, tonight—to take a bullet for him—that's a Roger, isn't it?

AGENT: *(Pause)* Repeat.

(The DOCTOR *grips the* AGENT's *shoulders. The* AGENT *is trembling.)*

DOCTOR: Because you're a brave young man, and you love what used to be your country—the remnant. And you love him, the man, you still love him—that's the truth.

AGENT: *(Shaking)* Decline to state.

DOCTOR: Steady. And you're a brave patriot who's sworn to help me bring him and this Country back to life—because you believe in the Resurrection and the Life, don't you, son?

AGENT: Repeat?

DOCTOR: And so does he. So does he. And that is why you have to help me bring him back to life. Because he's the son. He's the "Son of his Country." Because he's a death in our family. Because he knows deep in his dead heart that he was never really born, let alone born again; that he's only been a shadow and a sleepwalker and a cheerleader in other people's American nightmare. And you're going to help me raise him from the dead, right here, and when you do that then you, too, will be born again—because now, tonight, we are no longer in Florida—we are the last

two men in the United States of America! And we have
all the Power—John—*and all the responsibility!*

(The DOCTOR *braces the* AGENT. *They speak in strangled
tones.)*

DOCTOR: So, will you? —Will you—help me? Will you
give me the key to his wardrobe closet—where he
keeps his boots and his cowboy toys and costumes—
God help us! Will you? ...Is that a Roger, Mister Doe?!

AGENT: Repeat?

DOCTOR: *(Planting each word)* You have to dress him in
his cowboy costume—wait! —You have to give me that
key, because *if he dies—you are history!* There'll be no
one here. There's a hurricane coming—Hurricane
Xantippe, that mean anything to you? No. Well, trust
me when I tell you there's a shitstorm coming... He'll be
dead, the phones and the computers'll be down—I'll be
gone—country's been under martial law, in everything
but name only, for the last two years. We have lost our
Republic, sir! *Habeas Corpus* is gone, the "Great Writ"
is gone, with the wind, and there will be no one left to
"Produce the Body" ...And no one in Washngton D C,
the City of Lies, will know your name, Mister Doe...
So, tonight, you give me the key, and you do what you
have to, to shake him out of that stupor—and it's not an
act or a deception, you were right—wake him up before
this shitstorm hits, or get right away into that swamp
out there and I'll kill him myself, Texas style—before
they, "They", get him—*Homo Amerikanus,* the last of
his line—R I P. I will not let him linger. He will not be
tortured or tormented while I'm still here. Rest in Peace,
Mister Coe. *Do it*, Mister Doe—that's a Roger, Mister
Roe!

*(Silence, then the helicopter in and out, the chopper's beam
raking the office. Police dogs bark in the distance.)*

AGENT: Show me your I D...

DOCTOR: Repeat?

AGENT: Are you *a* certified M D?

DOCTOR: I told you: I was "Doctor Feelgood" —and
now I'm "Doctor Death". And you're "John Doe";
and his code-name was "Ranch Hand"—ha!—and also
"Commander in Chief": all lies, Mister Coe, except for
"Hurricane Xantippe" —that's her real name—in fact
the last truthful public utterance in this country took
place before you were born: Dallas, Texas, November
22, 1963: the President's wife, her name was Jacqueline
Kennedy, cried out after the *fifth* shot— "They've killed
my husband!"... They had. And she knew who "*They*"
were.

(The AGENT *backs into a deep shadow.)*

AGENT: ...Are you *a* illegal alien?

(The DOCTOR *turns out lamps: All moonlight, now.)*

DOCTOR: I'm the one who tells you who *you* are. *(Pause)*
Are you sitting down? ...You're a "sampling error."
An expendable statistic. Number One's last Praetorian
Guard. When he was turned into a national joke and
his poll numbers sank to one, you were the One. You
were with him when he snuck into Baghdad carrying a
plastic turkey in the dead of night, and you were there
to give him first aid when he ran over that policeman
on the golf links in Scotland, on that goddamn
bike—and most of all you were in Family Quarters
when the "Second Wave" hit Chicago on 2/13, and he
tried to kill himself on that same goddamn infernal—

AGENT: May-Day—Ranch Hand—May-Day!

(The AGENT *moves to confront the* DOCTOR. *Face to face in
front of the window, in moonlight.)*

DOCTOR: *(Overlapping)* ...And now they want us to do it:
You and me—the Spook and the Liberal—who love

him and hate him, respectively—so that, then, *They* can start all over again with the "Third Wave" or the "Reichstag Fire" or whatever they decide to call it next time.

AGENT: May-Day!

DOCTOR: Precisely. So you have to choose: between me and nothing. Because, Yes, like Doctor Frankenstein, I am a "certified" physician. And my first duty, as you may know, is to "do no harm." I've done enough "harm". I don't intend to do any more—unless you force me to it... But, as I say, I'll be gone. *(He opens the door.)* ...You can walk out—if you want to... You're free. So am I. That's the point. It comes down to us. You love the man. I hate him. That's what "They" are counting on: that you and I will kill each other and that he, yesterday's Hero of the Free World, will be cut down in the crossfire. You copy?

AGENT: Negative.

DOCTOR: *Then go!*

(The AGENT *marches to the door, then halts, drops to the floor and executes ten push-ups. Then he rises and stands as if trapped in the doorway, facing away from the* DOCTOR.*)*

DOCTOR: Good. You're preparing. Your body has a mind of it's own. So your three million year old body is stripping for action... Before your body decides what it's going to do, I want you to copy this:

(The psychoanalyst moves to the AGENT. *Stands behind and talks quietly into the younger man's ear.)*

DOCTOR: You and I have nothing in common. Nothing. Zero. Except that we each in our own way refuse to be slaves. I know you "copy" that. And that is why I do not believe that either of us is prepared to do "their" bidding. Now, if you will sit down, again, I will tell you, at last, just who "*They*" are.

(The DOCTOR *brings the two chairs center and he sits and waits. Mission bells. Then, the* AGENT *turns and walks very slowly to the facing chair.)*

DOCTOR: Thank you, son.

(But the AGENT *turns his chair directly away from the psychologist before sitting.)*

DOCTOR: That's good. You're getting ready to face *"Them."* ...Well— "They" are the "Undead" , the "Wise Men" of *The New York Times* together with their Academic battalions, and all their media rent-a-cops— who want Bush the Younger to be the scapegoat who takes the fall for all this horror, and allows us still another make-over so that *we* can be beautiful again... And I was one of them, Mister Coe—I gave them their psychological vitamin shots, and I helped the horror to happen. I am "Them" ...Now, we come to you, sir. *The New York Times* and I wanted a scapegoat, while you and Lord Rupert Murdoch and his Armies of the Right wanted a martyr. You were a Neo-Con dog face and you never knew it... That's about it. The Left wants an idiot in the family, while the Right looks for a traitor.

(The AGENT *does not respond. Low thunder building)*

DOCTOR: Are you sleeping? Agent Coe? *(Pause) Gun!*

AGENT: *Gun!*

(The AGENT, *still facing away, fans a phantom crowd with his gun, as in a dream.)*

DOCTOR: "Pump and Dump" —like Guantanamo. This was his *"Rendition!"* They dumped him here, like a goddamn vegetable, right here in Florida at the scene of the crime where the sons-of-bitches stole the presidency for him in the first place— Will you stand up, son, will you turn around, for Christ's sake!

(The AGENT *slowly turns in his chair; The* DOCTOR *faces the revolver.)*

DOCTOR: "...And the Madman cried, 'My name is Legion, for we are many...'"

(The DOCTOR'*s words stop the* AGENT; *he raises the pistol to his own head.)*

DOCTOR: "...And Jesus said, 'Come out of the man!'" ...But I'm not Jesus... We're not gods. We're not even human beings.

(The AGENT'*s gun hand falls.)*

AGENT: *(A murmur)* Negative.

DOCTOR: *(Looks up)* But we're here. And there's no one else... I'll do it—out of hatred for *"Them"*! But what I'm trying to tell you is that my hate and loathing for *"Them"* isn't enough. It's all over unless *you* can do something—out of *love for him!* —Do you copy?!

(The AGENT *stands, turns, faces the healer. The* DOCTOR *is near exhaustion. He limps close to the* AGENT.*)*

DOCTOR: I'm going to tell you your story, John Coe: You and all the other John Does—in your millions— loved him, and lived through him, and stepped forward to take the bullet for him—when it came. And, now, it's come, the bullet, the slow-motion bullet. And you have to take it for him. *Today.*

AGENT: May-Day?

DOCTOR: "May-Day"... You ready? ..."*Psycho-Drama!*"

AGENT: Repeat.

DOCTOR: "Psycho-Drama!" We're going to create a psycho-drama. You and I are going to be actors in a psychodrama. And we are going to strip him. We have to do that. Naked. You will go undercover. You will become a "cowboy," so that we—you and I—can get in

to the hell where he lives and unpack that bundle
of secrets. Listen carefully: I have taken him off his
medication. He will be in a state of nature. He will be
dangerous. Out of control. You may have to kill him....
You copy? I'll be with you, in this psycho-drama,
but you're the only one he trusts. You're the key.

AGENT: Repeat.

DOCTOR: ...The key?

(The AGENT *produces the key, the psychiatrist reaches for
it—but the guard does not, cannot, yet, let go. They stand,
each holding half of the key.)*

DOCTOR: I have a ninety-eight year-old mother out on
Key Largo. Twelve years ago, when *Time* magazine put
me on the cover with the "Ten Most Celebrated Healers
to the Sick and Famous," she, Mother, confided to me
that "this" —shitstorm—was coming. And then she,
of course, quoted Nietzsche: *(Thick Irish brogue)* "Boyo,
you are hangin' in dreams on the back of a tiger." And
then she moved right out to the Key to die. And that's
where I'll go, after the storm—and, then, *desaparacido.*
"Disappeared." You know all about that. But you won't
care about any of it because—unless you give me this
key—you'll be out there, naked, in the swamp, and the
jungle, hauling the dead body, of the Commander in
Chief, a half-step ahead of an *alligator* with jaws like
this—

(The DOCTOR *opens his arms wide, making alligator jaws.
The arm/jaws, in the moonlight, throw enormous shadows
on the adobe walls.)*

*(Mission bells toll midnight. Darkness on the frozen
AGENT—key still in hand.)*

Scene Two

(Six A M, six hours later; the DOCTOR *sleeps at his desk.
Through the window can be seen and heard the preliminary
and premonitory sounds and signs of the approaching
Hurricane: drizzle, black sky, low thunder, hot morning
wind, swaying palms, creaking wood, slamming doors.)*

(The DOCTOR *bolts up from his nightmare.)*

DOCTOR: Jesus Christ!

*(He gathers himself; turns on the radio. Low rumbling
thunder; Mission bells. He dials a number.)*

RADIO NEWS: ...Category 5, according to sources in the
Governor's office, where we will be going momentarily.
It is exactly eight minutes after six, Sunday, January 6th,
and while we're waiting, these headlines: London:
Former Secretary of State Condoleezza Rice, who has—

DOCTOR: *(Into telephone)* ...Mother? ..."Mayday"
...Mother? ..."Mayday!"

RADIO NEWS: ...been charged by the International Court
of Justice with—

*(The roar of the dirt bike wipes out the newscast. The
DOCTOR hangs up the telephone receiver, kills the radio,
speaks into a hand held tape recorder, as he hurries out, Left.)*

DOCTOR: *(Into tape)* Psycho-drama in progress—Patient
Number One is in the *hacienda*—6:08 A M—psychotic
pseudo-sexual episode now unfolding— Heroic
measures indicated for abreaction... *(Exits).*

*(The bike noise ratchets in, then out, followed by the sound of
two men shouting, laughing and singing.* AGENT *enters.)*

AGENT: C'MON, Sir, lead the way! Sir? C'mon *(Sings,
and plays toy guitar.)* "Home, home on the
range—Home, home..." *(He listens, then bolts off to find
the* PATIENT.*) Sir?!*

(Off, the sound of the unmedicated PATIENT *jumping out at
the* AGENT.*)*

PATIENT: *(Off)* Yee— Hah!

(Next, the two men stumble past the upstage window.
They are costumed in complete cowboy regalia, including
Stetson hats, boots and spurs, and toy guns for the madman.
They crash into and get stuck in the office door frame.)

PATIENT: Yee—hah! Get yo' behind in here, Bubba! This
here, is "DOC'S PLACE." I told you I knew where I was
goin', but, no, you don't believe me, *amigo*, you thought
your old *compañero* was lost, you figured I was all hat
and no cattle, thought I was plumb *loco (Leaps into office)*
—Ha! —Hey, Doc! —Wait'll you meet the Doc, he's—

AGENT: *(Louder)* Hey, Doc!

(Sound of flushing toilet, and the DOCTOR re-enters,
in a white medical coat. The PATIENT leaps back in terror
—he has yet to ever look the DOCTOR in the eye—then
pushes the AGENT in between himself and the alienist.)

PATIENT: *(Behind the AGENT)* —Hey, Doc! *Como esta,*
amigo. There's the Doc, Bubba—some say he's a Limey,
some say somthin' else—you know what I mean?
—But I say he's just ol' Doc Tequila and when you
get some of his white lightnin' inside you, *mi hermano,*
you'll, by God, know you're a *man.* 'Cause when you
hit home at old "Doc's", here, you are drinkin' with the
he-men!

(Again, the PATIENT and the DOCTOR try, respectively, to
avoid and to make contact. Then, the PATIENT and AGENT
suddenly glare at each other.)

PATIENT: Who you lookin' at?

AGENT: Who *you* lookin' at?

PATIENT: *(Beat)* I axed you first.

(DOCTOR confides into his hidden tape recorder:)

DOCTOR: "Paranoid homophobic scenario" underway...

AGENT: *(Pause)* Hey, Doc!

(The PATIENT *breaks the staring match: he feints toward the* AGENT's *groin.* AGENT *flinches;* PATIENT *yelps:)*

PATIENT: Yee-hah!

(Then, he grabs a small globe off the desk and begins a "football game" with the AGENT—*passing and running in extreme slow motion. The* PATIENT's *voice is transformed into the whiskey organ of an old time sportscaster.)*

PATIENT: *(As sportscaster and runner)* "...Texas A and M's ball on, this, the south side of the field. There's the snap and it's a handoff to Ray Whatley—and he's away, "Mister Outside" —downnnn to the twenty, to the tennn, to the five—

(The AGENT, *at a sign from the* DOCTOR, *makes a slow motion tackle of the* PATIENT *before he can injure himself. The two lie together, panting on the floor. Doors slam in the rising wind.)*

AGENT: ...Touchdown...

PATIENT: *(Happy as a child in grace)* ...Mission accomplished...

(The DOCTOR *gives thumbs up sign.)*

DOCTOR: Drinks are on the house, boys. *(He speaks into tape:)* "Aim-inhibited, Allo-Plastic, Acting Out of repressed Homoerotic hidden agenda—"

(The DOCTOR *breaks off as the two Football Boys rise from the floor and resume their roles as cowboys. Now, the two cowboys fill up the room, their body and vocal imagery transforming the office into a hole-in-the-wall rural bar: "DOC'S PLACE." The* DOCTOR *watches and waits. Low thunder.)*

PATIENT: *(Grabs* AGENT's *ass)* Say, Padner, put some *dinero* in that juke box. *Arriba!*

(The DOCTOR *nods to the* AGENT.*)*

AGENT: *(Miming the juke box)* Here you go.

PATIENT: Yes, sir. *(Listening in his head)* That's a good old tune.

(The DOCTOR *and the* AGENT *watch as the* PATIENT *stands still, listening in the low stormbound silence.)*

(Before the PATIENT *can drop out of the psycho- drama, the clinician takes up the toy guitar and begins a song:)*

DOCTOR: ...Who did you say it was, brother?...

(Pause, then the Cowboy President reacts in full voice:)

PATIENT: Who did you say it was, brother?

(Then, the PATIENT *sings to the* AGENT, *who joins in with him—brother to brother.)*

PATIENT & AGENT:
Who did you say it was, brother?
Who was it fell by the way?
When whiskey and blood run together
Did you hear anyone pray?

Their names I'm not able to tell you,
But here is one thing I can say:
There were whiskey and blood mixed together,
But I didn't hear nobody pray.

I didn't hear nobody pray, dear brother,
I didn't hear nobody pray.
I heard the crash on the highway,
But I didn't hear nobody pray.

(The analyst slips over to stand in and block the exit from the office, stage right.)

(As the PATIENT *begins to mime a fist fight, the* DOCTOR *signals the* AGENT *to block the other doorway, stage left.)*

PATIENT & AGENT:
Whiskey and glass all together,
Was mixed up with blood where they lay.
Death played her hand in destruction,
But I didn't hear nobody pray.

(Now the DOCTOR, *intervenes, adds his voice to the
rendition—pushes, gambles for the break-thru!)*

PATIENT, AGENT, &DOCTOR:
I didn't hear nobody pray, dear brother,
I didn't hear nobody pray.
I heard the crash on the highway,
But I didn't hear nobody pray.

(The DOCTOR *signals the* AGENT *to stop. The* PATIENT
*stomps some imagined opponent to death. Then, he sinks
to one knee, his hands held high above his head as if in
surrender. He sings on, alone.)*

PATIENT: *(Alone)*
Give up the game an' stop drinking,
For Jesus is pleading with you. It cost him a lot in
redeeming,
Redeeming the promise for you.

*(Slowly the healer crosses to the broken prisoner. The
PATIENT listens to the approaching steps, cowers, waits
for the axe to fall. Instead, the DOCTOR helps the PATIENT
to stand. Silence. Low storm sounds)*

DOCTOR: Alright, son—your turn.

(The DOCTOR *motions to the* AGENT *and both sit, down left
and down right, respectively.)*

PATIENT: *(Pause, then a tired Texas voice)* ...My name is,
uh, "George" —and I'm, uh, a alcoholic.

(The DOCTOR *nods to the* AGENT.*)*

DOCTOR & AGENT: Hi, George.

(So, now, the office is a quiet Alcoholics Anonymous, A A, meeting.)

PATIENT: ...And, uh, I've been sober, uh, going on, uh, about two weeks, here...

(The PATIENT is pale and trembling. This is the past, this happened. Low thunder.)

(The DOCTOR and the AGENT, each in his own way, are in the imagined or recalled scene with "George".)

PATIENT: ...so, like I told y'all last time—

DOCTOR: No. Stop. Tell the truth. Stop talking that "good ol' boy horseshit." You're a child of the Ivy League. Re-member who you are. *Re-member.*

(Frozen... The DOCTOR nods to the AGENT.)

AGENT: *(Softly, and saluting slowly)* You're the man—George.

(When the PATIENT speaks again, his voice and diction has the educated New England tinged tone of his long ago youth—reminiscent of the young John F Kennedy.)

PATIENT: ...Be myself? *(A smile)* "Mini-me"? My original nickname? "Junior"? "Shrub"? "Little George" and "George the Second"...or the one my mother invented when I...

DOCTOR: My God—Now he's Jack Kennedy...

(The smile fades. The boy hangs his head in shame. The DOCTOR signals the AGENT. The AGENT, in some pain, slowly crosses to the PATIENT and puts his arm around his shoulder.)

AGENT: *(A lump in his throat)* Affirmative.

(The AGENT resumes his seat.)

PATIENT: ...Anyway—hah—back then, when we first moved out, uh, West—my hero was Zorro and his

black horse. Because, you know, my Dad had all those
photos of himself as a star first baseman and a war
hero—so I told my mom that I wanted to be like my
Dad because he was, you know, a hero like Zorro—
And Mom, she, she—she had mint on her breath—she,
she laughed, she said, "Zorro? You mean *Zero*, don't
you? Your hero is *Zero*." Ho—ho, we all laughed...

(PATIENT, *the boy, is lost again. The* AGENT, *this time
without prompting, whispers to him.*)

AGENT: Affirmative.

(*The* PATIENT'*s mood begins to swing from humiliation to
rage: He mops his face, hugs himself for control.*)

PATIENT: "Horseshit"?The truth? Referring to Yale?
Referring to Skull & Bones? ...Here's what they did to
us—and you're never supposed to tell, but I don't give
a goddamn anymore. They—and I'm not lying now—
they make you strip buck naked, and all of you
"initiates" climb down, together, into a big black vat
of horseshit, hot horse manure, and they're, they, the
Old Boys, the Bonesmen are marching around the vat,
slow, dressed up like skeletons and they're chanting
in German, you know, "Die, die, die to the Bone..."
(*He sways, ready to vomit.*)

AGENT: (*whispers*) Repeat.

PATIENT: "Die..." Then— (*Fascist salute*) "Long live
Death!" ...And, ah, then you, ah, crawl out and they, ah,
wash you off, the Old Boys, and then they lay you—
they, ah, they lay you in a velvet coffin, and then, you
close your eyes and—later they sing a song about how,
now (*Chants*) "You're Born Again—into the Bone"
...And all the clocks—at Skull and Bones—they kept all
the clocks five minutes fast...why did they do that? No
one ever told me why they did that...

(And now, for the first time, the PATIENT *has the courage to finally turn and look directly at the* DOCTOR.)

(The wind moans. At length, the DOCTOR *signals to the* AGENT *and the two stand on either side of the ruined leader.)*

DOCTOR: Were you? Born again?

PATIENT: ...No.

AGENT: *(Softly)* Negative.

DOCTOR: No.

PATIENT: Later.

AGENT: *(Softly)* Repeat.

DOCTOR: When?

PATIENT: Christ Jesus.

AGENT: Amen.

DOCTOR: No... No. That was a lie... So, do it now.

PATIENT: Help.

DOCTOR: Really do it. Tell the truth. Finish it.

PATIENT: Help.

AGENT: Repeat.

DOCTOR: Tell the truth! Kneel down—or stand up: *just tell the truth!*

(The DOCTOR *backs away and gestures the* AGENT *to do the same.)*

PATIENT: Help!...Help! *(He tries, in vain, to kneel.)*

DOCTOR: You. You. Only *you.*

AGENT: That's a Roger.

(Alone, center, the PATIENT *reaches toward the other two, pleading for help.)*

PATIENT: *(To* AGENT*)* Help? *(To* DOCTOR*)* Help?

DOCTOR: *No! Don't touch him!* He has to do it—
(To the PATIENT*)* You have to do it, Son—of your
own free will— *You have to help yourselfon your
own—yousonofabitch—for once in your life!*

*(*DOCTOR *and* AGENT *struggle to keep from helping the
tortured fallen leader.)*

PATIENT: Help!

DOCTOR: No!

PATIENT: Help!

DOCTOR: Third time. Last chance, son.

(The AGENT *slowly kneels. Storm rising. The* DOCTOR
watches. Doors slam. The prisoner PATIENT *jerks as if shot.)*

(They wait for the PATIENT *to kneel. He tries. Fails. Tries.
Sways. Fails again. Wind rising. Thunder building)*

PATIENT: *(Crouching) Please!*

DOCTOR: *(To the* AGENT*)* Wait—he's alone, now.
(To the madman) Listen to me—Junior! —Listen:
Stand up—if you truly believe in this insane bloodbath
in the "Holy Land" —stand up! Get out—go there—
yourself, and fight and die, with the poor bastards that
you lied and tricked into that hell on earth—

PATIENT: *Help me—*

DOCTOR: I *am!* I am helping you. *(To the* AGENT*)* He's all
alone now—back off! *(To the broken cowboy)* I'm telling
you to stand up, or get down on your knees—get down
and beg the world for your life—and never, ever, use
the words "Jesus Christ" or "Democracy" again!

PATIENT: *(Searching for God) Help!*

DOCTOR: *Kneel down! —Or stand up! You sonofabitch, you!*

(The PATIENT *makes his final effort. The* AGENT*'s lips now
move in fervent prayer.)*

AGENT: ...Forgive us our trespasses...

(The DOCTOR *is willing the* PATIENT, *the war criminal, to stand or to kneel; and he, the war-torturer, in a torque of agony, at war with his own body, in the last extreme of torture, makes one final heroic effort in his birth pangs, as the* DOCTOR *groans.)*

DOCTOR: Do it, you sonofabitch...

(He—the boy, the bones-man, the world-criminal—he, cannot kneel, cannot kneel or stand to be born again— too late.)

PATIENT: ...*Daddy—help me...kill me—Daddy!*

AGENT: ...yea, though I walk through the Valley of the Shadow of Death, I will fear no evil...

*(*AGENT *sobs silently. The* DOCTOR *pants, exhausted, finally. Mission bells, far away, then louder thunder. The* PATIENT—*the executioner and the victim in one wracked and striated body—pulls himself away, at last, and stumbles toward the door. He has become an old man.)*

(In the doorway, Right, he twists up into his former fake cowboy image. And when he speaks, the voice and diction are, once again, the hollow, vicious braggadocio of his former false self—yet the lost boy still calls out from within.)

PATIENT: ...*(To the* AGENT*)* Bubbaaaah! —let's hit the trail—*Arriba!* Get-um-up, Scout— Let's ride, Ranger! *(To his* DOCTOR/*Father)* So long, P— P— Pappy...*hasta la vista,* Doc!

(Completely lost in his damnation, he whirls out into the storm, whooping raw "rebel yells.")

(The DOCTOR *limps center, cursing:)*

DOCTOR: Sonofabitch.

(The AGENT *crawls to him, praying.)*

(Far away, a storm warning bell—then, outside, the roar of the madman's motor bike and his ghastly rebel yells merge into the fury of the hurricane along with the cries and curses of the AGENT *and the* DOCTOR:)

AGENT	DOCTOR:
...Now I lay me down to,	Sonofabitch—
sleep, I pray the lord my	Sonofabitch—
soul to keep— If I should	Goddamnsonofabitch—
die before I wake...	Sonofabitchsonofabitch—
I pray the Lord—	*I'm a*
Help— Help— Help!...	*SonofaGoddamnsonofabitch!...*

(With the AGENT's *final cry for help he is clinging to the* DOCTOR—*like a child to a parent, like the Fool to King Lear in the storm. Then, a sudden silence as the gale sinks momentarily.)*

AGENT: P—P—P—P...

DOCTOR: *(A murmur)* I'm-a-son...

(Doors slam, again, like gun shots, and the storm spikes with a howl drowning out the two. The lips of the men move, unheard, in the raging slamming hurricane.)

(Then—over all the sound and fury—the remorseless and terrific chopping of the giant helicopter.)

END OF PLAY

www.ingramcontent.com/pod-product-compliance
Lightning Source LLC
Chambersburg PA
CBHW070031110426
42741CB00035B/2730

* 9 7 8 0 8 8 1 4 5 3 4 9 2 *